CRITICALLY ENDANGERED ANIMALS

WHAT ARE THEY?

ANIMAL BOOKS FOR KIDS
Children's Animal Books

BABY PROFESSOR
EDUCATION KIDS

Speedy Publishing LLC
40 E. Main St. #1156
Newark, DE 19711
www.speedypublishing.com

The more people there are in the world, the more we take over wild space for buildings and roads, and to grow food. Our activities also change the Earth's climate. These things make it harder for some animals to survive. Read on and learn about species of animals at risk.

A confrontation between two White Rhino.

ANIMALS AT RISK

Many animal species are *"threatened"* or *"at risk"*. This may be because their habitat is disappearing, because of the effects of pollution or global warming, or because people hunt them so much for food or just as trophies. A species is declared *"at risk"* when scientists note that the number of animals has been dropping steeply for a long time, and has gotten so low that the species may not survive without help and protection.

Scientists try to keep track of species that are at risk, and share what they know so people and governments can take steps to make it possible for species to survive.

This does not always work. Since 1900, almost 500 animal species have become extinct. Almost all of these extinctions are directly or indirectly caused by human activity.

Scientists have three general categories for species at risk: **Vulnerable, Endangered,** and **Critically Endangered.**

Breaching Humpback Whale.

A group of Walrus relaxing on the ice near the water.

VULNERABLE SPECIES

A vulnerable species faces threats where it naturally lives that may wipe it out over time. These threats may include over-hunting and loss of their natural habitat. A vulnerable species is not going to disappear in the next couple of years, but if circumstances don't change it will be in danger soon.

H ere are some vulnerable species from all over the world. Some of them have wonderful names!

- **Wandering Albatross**

- **Giant Anteater**

- **Common Eland**

- **Four-Horned Antelope**

- **Asian Black Bear**

- **Siamese Fighting Fish**

Galapagos Tortoise.

- Secretary Bird

- Clouded Leopard

- Galapagos Tortoise

- Golden Hamster

- Lion

- Manta Ray

- California Sea Lion

Giant Anteater in nature.

- **Great White Shark** (learn more about these amazing fish in the Baby Professor book *The Great White Shark*)

- **Spectacled Bear**

- **Pancake Tortoise**

- **Wallaby**

- **Walrus**

- **Yak**

- **Black-Billed Whistling Duck**

Asian Black Bear.

Portrait of a Western Lowland Gorilla.

ENDANGERED SPECIES

Populations of endangered species are dropping so quickly that they are at risk of extinction soon. Here are some examples:

BALD EAGLE

DDT, a pesticide that used to be in common use, has a chemical that causes the shells of eggs to become thin. That means more eggs crack before the baby bird can hatch, lowering the birth rates in many bird species. Stopping use of the pesticide, and other efforts, have helped preserve this species for now.

Bald Eagle.

SWIFT FOX

In the 1930s and 1940s in the United States and Canada, farmers and ranchers tried to reduce the number of wolves and coyotes. Their methods also almost wiped out the swift fox, which now only appears in less than half of its former habitat.

Swift Fox.

PEREGRINE FALCON

Like the eagles, the falcons have suffered from weakened shells to their eggs so many fewer babies were born. The species is making a slow recovery now that DDT is no longer widely in use.

Peregrine Falcon.

AMERICAN ALLIGATOR

Alligators are hunted for their meat and skin, and because people fear them as predators. As the human population grows in the southern United States, the alligator habitat decreases. Heavy conservation efforts are helping keep the alligators from disappearing altogether.

Basking American Alligator.

CALIFORNIA CONDOR

The California condor was almost wiped out by the chemicals in DDT that also attacked eagle and falcon eggs, as mentioned. They are carrion eaters, so they also suffer from lead poisoning when they eat carcasses of animals that have been killed with lead bullets. Condors frequently collide with power lines, and many die this way. There are fewer than 500 California condors left, half of them in captivity.

California Condor at Grand Canyon National Park.

FLORIDA PANTHER

Each male panther uses about 200 square miles as a hunting territory, and from that area feeds himself, between two and five females, and their young. Panther habitat in Florida has shrunk so dramatically that there were probably fewer than 20 panthers living outside of animal reserves and zoos in the 1970s.

Florida Panther stares intensely at camera close up.

The population has moved back up to over 150 through conservation efforts, but that number is so small that a single new challenge, such as climate change due to global warming, could end this species very quickly. Panthers die from collisions with cars and illnesses, and are weakened because of inbreeding and contact with industrial chemicals and fertilizers.

Endangered Florida Panther.

CRITICALLY ENDANGERED SPECIES

Species that are critically endangered have declined so far that there are almost no animals of the species left outside of zoos or wildlife preserves. There are so few individuals that animals have trouble finding mates and rearing their young.

For some species, there are efforts to take animals born and raised in captivity and re-introduce them into their traditional habitats; but for many species, most of their habitat no longer exists because of the spread of cities and farm lands.

Here are some critically-endangered species:

WHITE RHINOCEROS

This species has been on Earth for 15 million years, but today there are only five adults left in the wild. That is down from about 2,000 in 1960.

JAVAN RHINOCEROS

This species lives on the Indonesian main island, Java. It is dark gray and has a single horn. The folds of its skin make it look like it is wearing armor. There are fewer than 40 Javan rhinos left outside of zoos and refuges now, due to hunting and loss of habitat.

Wild African White Rhino, South Africa.

SUMATRAN TIGER

Poaching and cutting down the forests on the Indonesian island of Sumatra have reduced the habitat of these tigers to just a few remainders of forests, and there are only 400 or so Sumatran tigers left outside of zoos and preserves.

WESTERN LOWLAND GORILLA

The population of this species of gorilla, which lives in the Congo in Africa, has declined by 60% in the past twenty-five years due to disease, poaching, and loss of habitat.

Baby of a Western Lowland Gorilla.

AMUR LEOPARD

These leopards are solitary hunters in eastern Russia. Human activity has dramatically reduced their habitat, so just over 50 Amur leopards now survive outside of captivity.

HAWKSBILL TURTLE

These turtles have lived in all the oceans of the world for over 100 million years. They help keep coral reefs and beds of seagrass healthy. They are hunted for their pretty shells.

Hawksbill Sea Turtle close-up.

SOUTH CHINA TIGER

People hunted these tigers and killed thousands before the Chinese government moved to protect them in 1979. There may be fewer than 50 left in the wild.

PANGOLIN

Pangolins are weird creatures with armor made of scales. People hunt them for their scales and for their meat, and two of the eight pangolin species in Africa and Asia are almost extinct.

South China Tiger.

YANGTZE FINLESS PORPOISE

These porpoises are as intelligent as gorillas and live in the Yangtze River in China. There are only about one thousand left, because of pollution and other human activity.

Finless Porpoise.

SUMATRAN ORANGUTAN

The orangutans once lived all over the Indonesian island of Sumatra. They eat fruit and play a major part in the forest system by distributing the seeds of fruit over their territory. Due to the loss of habitat, hunting, and poaching to sell to orangutans as pets, there are just a few groups of orangutans left in isolated forest areas in the north of the island.

Sumatran Orangutan.

NORTHERN BALD IBIS

These beautiful birds, which used to live all along the north coast of Africa and the western Middle East, now only survive in a few areas of Morocco and Syria. There are fewer than 300 birds left, although the population has grown slightly in the past decade.

Bald Ibis preening.

GUAM RAIL

Guam rails are flightless birds that lived on Guam Island in the Pacific Ocean. When brown tree snakes came to the island, they almost wiped out the birds. Today, almost all of the species live in captivity in Guam and in the United States. There is a project to introduce the rails back into wild areas of Guam.

Guam Rail at the Cincinnati Zoo.

NORTHERN HAIRY-NOSED WOMBAT

These Australian mammals were thought to be extinct, but in the 1930s a small group of about 150 wombats were discovered in Queensland. Efforts continue to protect their habitat.

BLACK-FOOTED FERRETS

There are now fewer than 1000 black-footed ferrets in North American, although they once lived throughout the prairies. They are under threat from disease and loss of habitat.

Black-footed Ferret.

WHITE ANTELOPE

This species, also known as the Addax antelope, has lived for thousands of years in the Sahara desert. Habitat destruction and over-hunting have reduced the population to fewer than 200 animals.

VAQUITA

These rare marine mammals look like porpoises and live along the Pacific coast of Mexico. They are often caught in the nets used for illegal fishing in the area, and are killed or left to drown. Fewer than 100 vaquita still exist in the wild.

Addax Antelope.

CARING FOR THE WHOLE EARTH

Some people call our Earth *"Gaia"*, a single organism. Learn about our home, and all the species and natural wonders that you are connected to, in other Baby Professor books like *Peeling the Earth Like an Onion, The Endangered Mammals from Around the World, Who Lives in the Barren Desert?,* and *Insects and Arachnids.*

Visit

BABY PROFESSOR
EDUCATION KIDS

www.BabyProfessorBooks.com
to download Free Baby Professor eBooks
and view our catalog of new and exciting
Children's Books

Made in the USA
Coppell, TX
27 October 2022

85335055R00040